$5.00

D0592183

Learning by Discovery

LEARNING BY DISCOVERY:

A CRITICAL APPRAISAL

Lee S. Shulman
Evan R. Keislar
Editors

Proceedings of a conference on Learning
by Discovery under the sponsorship of
Stanford University and the Committee on
Learning and the Educational Process of the
Social Science Research Council. The con-
ference was conducted and reported pur-
suant to a contract with the United States
Department of Health, Education, and
Welfare, Office of Education, under the pro-
visions of the Cooperative Research Program.

RAND MCNALLY & COMPANY   CHICAGO

RAND McNALLY EDUCATION SERIES

B. Othanel Smith *Advisory Editor*

Broudy and Palmer, *Exemplars of Teaching Method*
Broudy, Smith, and Burnett, *Democracy and Excellence in American Secondary Education*
Burns and Lowe, *The Language Arts in Childhood Education*
Dupuis, *Philosophy of Education in Historical Perspective*
Farwell and Peters, eds., *Guidance Readings for Counselors*
Foshay, ed., *Rand McNally Handbook of Education*
Hains, *Guiding the Student Teaching Process in Elementary Education*
Kaplan and Steiner, *Musicianship for the Classroom Teacher*
Kimbrough, *Political Power and Educational Decision-Making*
Krumboltz, ed., *Learning and the Educational Process*
Lewenstein, *Teaching Social Studies in Junior and Senior High Schools*
Lieberman and Moskow, *Collective Negotiations for Teachers*
Litwack, Holmes, and O'Hern, *Critical Issues in Student Personnel Work*
Michaelis, ed., *Teaching Units in the Social Sciences*, 3 volumes
Norris, Zeran, and Hatch, *The Information Service in Guidance*, 2nd edition
Parker, ed., *Rand McNally Curriculum Series*
    Ford and Pugno, eds., *The Structure of Knowledge and the Curriculum*
    Parker and Rubin, *Process as Content*
    Wellington and Wellington, *The Underachiever*
Perrodin, ed., *The Student Teacher's Reader*
Peters and Farwell, *Guidance: A Developmental Approach*
Peters, Shertzer, and Van Hoose, *Guidance in Elementary Schools*
Phi Delta Kappa, *Education and the Structure of Knowledge*
Phi Delta Kappa, *Improving Experimental Design and Statistical Analysis*
Rollins and Unruh, *Introduction to Secondary Education*
Shulman and Keislar, eds., *Learning by Discovery*
Smith, ed., *Aesthetics and Criticism in Art Education*
Smith and Ennis, eds., *Language and Concepts in Education*
Taba and Elkins, *Teaching Strategies for the Culturally Disadvantaged*
Trump and Baynham, *Focus on Change: Guide to Better Schools*
Vassar, ed., *Social History of American Education*, 2 volumes
Wolf and Loomer, *The Elementary School: A Perspective*
Zeran and Riccio, *Organization and Administration of Guidance Services*

Also published by Rand McNally,
    Gage, ed., *Handbook of Research on Teaching*—A Project of the American Educational
        Research Association

Preface

SINCE ITS ORGANIZATION IN 1962, THE COMMITTEE ON LEARNING AND the Educational Process of the Social Science Research Council has been active in fostering research in the area of the application of psychology to education. It has arranged a conference on the perceptual and linguistic aspects of reading, and two six-week summer conferences (one in 1964 and one in 1965) for the training of educational research workers, largely at the postdoctoral level.

In February of 1964 the committee decided to initiate a conference on the topic of *learning by discovery*, the proceedings of which are reported in the present volume. The conference, held in New York City, January 28 and 29, 1965, was sponsored by the U.S. Office of Education in cooperation with Stanford University. It was held in order to (1) clarify some of the issues involved; (2) review what is now known about this subject; and (3) suggest ways of extending knowledge in this field.

The members of the committee during 1964 and 1965 included Lee J. Cronbach, Stanford University, chairman; Eleanor J. Gibson, Cornell University; Richard Atkinson, Stanford University; Evan R. Keislar, University of California, Los Angeles; George A. Miller, Harvard University; Lloyd N. Morrisett, Carnegie Corporation of New York, and Judson C. Shaplin, Washington University, St. Louis. Ben Willerman served as staff for the committee until his death in 1965, when he was replaced by Rowland L. Mitchell, Jr.

The subcommittee delegated to plan the conference included Evan Keislar, chairman; Robert Gagné, American Institute for Research, Pittsburgh; and Jerome Kagan, Harvard University. Lee S. Shulman, Michigan State University, was appointed recorder for the conference.

v

In addition to the members of the committee and subcommittee, the following individuals participated in the conference: Jerome Bruner, Harvard University; Robert Davis, The Madison Project, Webster College, St. Louis, Missouri; Robert Glaser, University of Pittsburgh; David Hawkins, University of Colorado; Robert Karplus, University of California, Berkeley; Howard H. Kendler, University of California, Santa Barbara; Bert Y. Kersh, Center for Teaching Research, Monmouth, Oregon; Sonia Osler, The Johns Hopkins Hospital; Walter R. Reitman, University of Michigan; Lee S. Shulman, Michigan State University; Michael Wallach, Duke University; Sheldon H. White, University of Chicago; David Wiley, University of California, Los Angeles; Merlin C. Wittrock, University of California, Los Angeles; Rowland L. Mitchell, Jr., Social Science Research Council. Observers included J. Richard Suchman, U.S. Office of Education; Charles Whitmer, National Science Foundation; Rosslyn Suchman, Office of Naval Research and Gallaudet College, Washington, D.C.

Appreciation is expressed to the U.S. Office of Education for its sponsorship of the conference, under Project No. F-064, in cooperation with Stanford University as contracting agent, and to the staff of the Social Science Research Council, who made the physical arrangements for the conference. We are also indebted to Roslyn Blum and Carolyn Stern for helpful suggestions with respect to revisions in the manuscript, to Joyce Stewart for her transcriptions of the many audio-tapes of conference discussions and her typing of the final manuscript, and to Joan Lynas for her assistance in the preparation of the bibliography and index. We also thank Clara Hahne for her administrative services before, during, and after the conference.

Lee S. Shulman
Evan R. Keislar

East Lansing, Michigan
Los Angeles, California
March, 1966

Contents

Introduction

THIS VOLUME IS DIVIDED INTO FIVE MAJOR SECTIONS. THE FIRST SECTION
deals with the dimensions of the issue of *learning by discovery*. In his
paper, David Hawkins takes the position that there are certain kinds of
things that can be learned only by discovery. Among them are those
experiences which constitute the preparation process in any learning
sequence. He also argues that in education, as in many other practical
sciences, the art of the practitioner is often capable of producing effects
which the theoretician is still at a loss to explain. Robert Glaser looks
at the question of discovery in the direct terms of the psychologist concerned with problems of training. His implication, vis-a-vis Hawkins, is
that when an objective is described in behavioral terms, the behavior is
clearly teachable.

The second section of the volume deals with the educational and
psychological research pertaining to discovery. M. C. Wittrock reviews
the literature of research in "The Learning by Discovery Hypothesis."
By so doing, he attempts to clarify some of the confusion which has
pervaded the field. In "The Logic of Experiments on Discovery," Lee
Cronbach presents a critical analysis of research, not only on learning by
discovery, but in the general field of education itself. He is especially
critical of the constricted range of dependent variables typically utilized
in learning experiments and suggests a dramatic increase in their number and scope.

The third section focusses upon attempts to utilize ideas generated
by the concept of learning by discovery in curricular innovations. In his
article, Jerome Bruner describes the activities of classes engaged in some
unique approaches to the social sciences. He presents a number of vivid
examples of children making discoveries and attempts to enumerate a

list of elements which account for what takes place in the classroom. "Discovery in the Teaching of Mathematics" finds Robert Davis discussing the way in which notions of learning by discovery have influenced the objectives and execution of the Madison project, one of the 'new mathematics' curricula. Both papers in this section focus on what teachers do.

The fourth section deals with psychological research and theory and their implications for the practice of education. In "Varieties of Learning and the Concept of Discovery," Robert M. Gagné utilizes his hierarchical model of kinds of learning as a tool for analyzing the relevance of the concept of discovery in learning. "Learning, Attention, and the Issue of Discovery" is Jerome Kagan's analysis of the personological or, as he prefers to call them, parapsychological variables in learning by discovery. Kagan emphasizes the developmental and individual-difference variables which must be taken into consideration before evaluation of any principle of learning can take place.

The final section of the volume is composed of reflections, further reflections, and a retrospective analysis. In their papers, Howard Kendler and Lloyd Morrisett review and analyze the preceding papers in an on-the-spot operation which took place in the final session. In "The Problem of Discovery: Conference in Retrospect," Evan Keislar and Lee Shulman utilize the advantages of time and their editorial opportunity to study the papers to present a retrospective analysis of the conference and a prospectus for future research in this area. Since the same sources were so frequently cited by different authors, a common bibliography for all the papers is presented at the end of the book.

At the end of each of the first four sections is a summary of the discussions which took place immediately following the presentation of each paper. Summarizing discussions by a group of psychologists, physical scientists, philosophers, and educators, carried on over a two-day period, is a task which admits of a number of strategies. Reporting verbatim the words of the discussants has the distinct advantage of preserving the dramatic impact of assertion and confrontation; however, it has the concomitant disadvantage of discontinuity and disorganization invariably present when any group of individuals is engaged in active debate.

An alternative strategy is to ignore the actual sequence of positions taken and simply to present, in most distilled form, the gist of statements made by members of the group in any discussion as these are appropriate to a specified topic.

In this volume a compromise procedure was adopted. We decided to preserve, whenever possible, the dramatic and dialectical advantages of reporting the confrontation between ideas, while introducing greater order and homogeneity of content into the summarized discussions. To do this required modifying the order in which various conversations occurred, while maintaining the feeling of dialogue in the interchanges. It is hoped that, in this form, the volume will serve the needs of its readers more adequately, just as a history is more valuable than a simple chronicle. The various positions taken by the participants on the topic of, for example, language and discovery, may have spanned all five sessions of the conference. For purposes of this volume, however, all these statements and rebuttals are gathered together in a single session, as if they had occurred contiguously. Whenever this procedure might have produced a distortion, the original context was retained. Hence, the discussion sections represent a mating of academic responsibility and editorial license. The license, however, is taken only with sequence, never with content.

PART ONE

THE ISSUE

Chapter I

Learning the Unteachable

DAVID HAWKINS

IN THIS PAPER I HAVE TWO PARALLEL INTERESTS. THE FIRST IS THE investigative art which we adults practice who are interested in the furtherance of education; here I shall try to speak partly as a philosopher of science. The second is to report, by a few small examples, a particular kind of investigation into the investigative art as practiced by children of elementary school age.

The art we are engaged in, as I see it, is a potentially fruitful combination of the practical and the scientific. We hope to contribute some real guidance to the evolution of educational systems, primarily through learning some significant things about the psychology of learning and of teaching. Our efforts are being made, I believe, in an historical situation where the best practice excels the best theory in quite essential ways; this fact defines a strategy we ought to follow.

There have often been times in the history of science when the personal knowledge of practitioners was significantly deeper than anything embedded in the beliefs and writings of the academically learned. Indeed, science has never started in a social vacuum, but has grown typically out of the interplay of *Theorizein* and those practically achieved mappings of nature embodied in the working arts. There is an amusing example in the mathematical theory of probability. It is recorded by Suetonius that the Emperor Claudius wrote a treatise on the art of dicing. The Roman and Greek form of the game, still played in England I think, involved three throws of three dice, each ranging in score from aces to boxcars ('dog' to 'Venus'). In the Middle Ages, gentlemen and ladies played vigorously, and there were schools of theory and strategy. Yet, with the exception of unimportant anticipations, we can date the beginning of combinatoric *theory* from the famous conversation of Pascal with the good Chevalier de Mérée. What every soldier of the Legion knew a good bit about from his *tesserai* had to

3

wait two thousand years for the literal breakthrough into the camp of the learned—a break through a wall of social insulation; and because of the relevance to the flourishing mathematics of Pascal's day, it was not long before a mathematician would know more about the subject than any mere gentleman. Part of the explanation, of course, is social onus. De Moivre had to apologize in his preface for writing about it at all.

As another example, there is the story of Gilbert, who has a deserved fame in the history of physics because he had the wit and intellectual courage to seek instruction concerning the magnet from metallurgists, mariners, and miners, rather than rest content with his tradition.

Of course the situation is never twice the same, in any detail, and our situation is more complex, but I think it justifies the analogy and thus suggests directions.

I have, and want only, to speak personally in the first instance. The good teaching I have observed, teaching by teachers who are accustomed to major success, owes little to modern theories of learning and cognition and much to apprenticeship, on-the-job inquiry, discussion, trial—ceaseless trial—within a common-sense psychological framework; a framework that is not all unsophisticated, however, and is able to accept individual insights from psychological (mostly psychotherapeutic) sources but without jargon or dogma: keeping the practice dry.

I would say also that the difference between the best teaching and the worst, or even the average, is very great. I conjure up a measure which would scale about like the distribution of billiard scores, not normal but skewed, even logarithmically skewed, and for the reasons that generally underly the logarithmico-normal distributions: something that increases its accommodation with its growth.

Under these circumstances, it seems to me the better part of wisdom to find the good school situations—not the better third but the best one per cent—and engage in close observation and intellectual resonance; then to try to recreate such situations and make them more abundant and reproducible, no holds barred. Nothing about this process is easy, but it can be done because it *is* done—but rarely. Nor is formal codification a first or a safe step. The essence is certainly not a simple one; more than likely it is a subtle mapping across conspicuous variations in local culture and individual style. However difficult the formulation, there are in practice many ways by which one can recognize good school situations without consulting or writing a formulary. We all know some of them, and probably none knows all of them. The best at it are likely to be those who practice the art and are articulate, can talk back to academics; so the initial role of the latter is necessarily and enjoyably a humble one. In fact, this first direction of research is co-extensive with some kinds of practical innovative work that many of us have begun to engage in, sometimes, I think, with too prompt a closure as to our goals.

This may turn out to be the kind of talk which will leave me in the position of a speaker who was constrained to finish by saying, "Now, if there is anyone I haven't insulted, I apologize." I expose my own breast, if that helps. At any rate, I want to expose my own belief, surely based on inadequate evidence, that most experimental work in the psychology of learning and teaching has not been very relevant to learning or teaching. A teacher friend of mine put it thus: "Most psychologists," she said, "have never really *looked* at children." Since of course most psychologists, and certainly all those here, *have* obviously looked at children, the remark may need some interpretation.

To interpret: Let me say something first about the concept of *preparation*, as when one talks about preparing an experiment. I do not mean the preparation which consists in getting oneself ready, but the preparation of the subject of the experiment, a light-beam, or a colony of paramoecia, or a child, or classroom of children. In physics or in chemistry of a classical sort, the preparation in this sense is what one does by arranging boundary conditions—by isolating and controlling—or in observing them; it does not matter in one sense, except the boundary conditions relevant to testing a particular hypothesis may be almost infinitely rare in the wild state. In the modern range of physics the concept gets a sharper meaning, because to get a system in an antecedently well defined state involves choice, and thus a sacrifice: To achieve definition, i.e., preparation, the experimenter must introduce discontinuities in his knowledge of the system's past, must give up information conjugate to what he has gained in the preparation. In psychological investigation this is always likewise true in principle, though we have no firm formulations of it. In atomic physics, to compensate, we are usually dealing with relatively simple systems, and the preparation requires no long history—other than that of science itself.

There are many psychological experiments, I know, which require comparatively simple preparation; and good sampling across the relevant dimensions of a universe will sometimes help to reduce uncertainty in wild or unanticipated variables. So we settle for some kind of statistical preparation. Problems of control are more or less solved if we do not demand too much, and others can get more or less similar results. What

5

I want to say, however, is that the preparation involved in pedagogical investigations goes up very sharply with the significance of their results and that an experiment which takes a half-hour or a day or a week to prepare is, in general, not worth doing.

There is a fundamental theory about experiments; it comes out of physics and is relevant here, not because we are doing physics but because whatever we are doing is done in a physical milieu and not in a world of abstractions. To call something an independent variable is not to use a name but to claim an achievement. To do experiments in the high-energy physics of very small, things, for example, one must have apparatus whose large size can be specified in advance, from purely dimensional considerations. In biology another dimension looms as crucial, that is preparation time. To put a complex system in a prepared state takes time. The good biological experiments have such a long preparation time that husbandry becomes the dominant characteristic of a lab or station; in the short run, at least, its resident prepared species determine its experiments. And let us not forget that the greatest achievements of 19th-century biology were essentially opportunistic in their methodology, exploratory rather than experimental. I know some of the exceptions and I do not want to oversimplify, but that is the general picture.

In theory there is a natural measure of *amount* of preparation and, derivatively, of preparation time. It is the logarithm of the improbability of the prepared state in the milieu from which the sample is drawn, molecule, or paramoecium, or child, or classroom, or school. Judged by this standard, situations of optimal learning require a great deal of preparation. If we do experiments in learning with only superficial preparation—instructions, 'training,' etc., of short duration—then the rare things get swamped by statistical noise, the tail of the distribution is invisible. Whatever its limitations, the work of Piaget has the relevance it has because of a relatively long preparation for the observations resulting; and I am sure an even longer preparation is needed to get past some of the limitations of such work, including possible errors of interpretation, etc. But this is the other side of the picture from the usual complaint about lack of statistical methodology. The latter *alone*, with perfunctory preparation, will bury the Piaget phenomena. This brings me back to the point that looking for optimal teaching situations 'in the wild,' and seeking to stabilize and reproduce them, is an easier start than trying to create them de novo. The lack of this I see as the greatest stumbling block in a 'scientific' approach, and the commitment to it as a great scientific hope. Let us take, as a practical unit, the work of an optimal teacher in involving a whole class of children before he, as a teacher, is ready to harvest any impressive results. These times are automatically months at least, and for some purposes, years—lifetimes. If I am right in this, it means that the now standard image of the lab or clinic is inappropriate. It means that investigators in this area will look rather like teachers, or educational innovators, or classroom ethologists spending months watching preparations or 'doing' them and— to come back to my teacher friend's complaint—finally, "really looking at children."

Considered realistically, the preparatory art in this field will never be a simply programmed procedure, for the reason that each subject, whether four-year-old or college student, will differ in some important ways from all the others, and that there will of necessity be an artful intermixture of observation, diagnosis, treatment all along the way, tailored in some critical respects to each subject. It is of, course, most unlikely that different children will arrive at any predetermined point by the same pathway, or at the same time; on any cross section of a group, in any record of performance, there will be a large variance. It is this variance, or some part of it, which is often stereotyped and quantified as 'ability,' importing into the description of learning dubious assumptions not only of constancy but especially of linearity, without which the dispositional concept of ability becomes ill-defined.

You may have been troubled already as to what I mean by the contrast of preparation and experiment. The experiment is simply the injection of some specified material for learning, at a point when it is judged, by whatever criteria, that children have been brought to a state of preparation, or of momentary readiness, to have educationally interesting and significant interactions with it.

Let me give an example from the background of elementary school science in the middle grades. Very often in the study of physical systems, there is some real point, both literal and figurative, which has to be identified in order that sharp physical analysis can get under way. One of these is with the Archimedean balance, say a board on a stabilizing fulcrum with blocks for weights. This is a system which children can encounter, with interesting results, over a wide range of ages. But let us suppose we are in the range of the sort of result which Archimedes immortalized, the law of the unequal arm balance. I shall not even try to enumerate the learning preconditions that make this an educationally hopeful encounter. One is that children have a rule-schema already established; they are *looking for* a rule of balance. There are many interesting phenomena here, including 'wrong' rules that work very well over a variety of cases. I shall single out only one, which is that children often measure in to the blocks, from the ends of the board, rather than outward from the center of support. You can easily suppress this phenomenon of end-measuring if you want to. The point is that you *don't* want to; it is part of the definition of a prepared state. Suppose you encourage a tabulation of balanced configurations. Can a rule be extracted from this tabulation that will enable you to predict new balance configurations? Of course, since there is a simple transformation from one coordinate system into the other. Try end-measuring with equal numbers of blocks on the two sides, and you'll get a pretty obvious rule. Now try it with unequal numbers. The case is rather like that of the Ptolemaic-Copernican transformations, and for similar reasons. From our point of view there is a shadow parameter, like the Ptolemaic deferent: the half-length of the board. But from the child's point of view it is no shadow, the ends of the board are real natural markers, and he is accustomed to using their like in many other manipulations, physical and intellectual. To ask him to disregard them would be to remove a reliable conceptual tool, without replacing it. The pedagogical experiment, then, is to define empirically a set of pathways by which children will *discover* the possibilities of a fulcrum-centered coordinate system. Some children will have gotten it first, without any interest in the ends of the board. They are out of this particular game. Some will not make the transition, in spite of the preparation; those the experimenters will come back to, in another context. Some will make the transition only because 'teacher told them to.' Here the experiment is simply spoiled. But some will make it—if the preparation has been artful, and right. These we watch carefully, and listen to their discourse, perhaps taking some part in it as stabilizers and amplifiers. What were the paths? One might be some analogy to other centered systems i.e., tall block houses, or trees; preparation cannot exclude this variance, it is of the essence of experience. Another might be from accidental or contrived asymmetry of the board itself, with an extra weight to balance. A third might be from mapping the real board into the realm of tabulated numbers, then 'seeing' what we would call the linear transformation; some children have this early comfort with number-schemata. (But no one will see the world in a number line unless he has first *seen* the world.) A fourth will have been passive, but gotten the idea by contagion from a classmate. What has happened here? How does this differ from being told, by book or teacher?

A negative purpose in such experiments is to probe for the limits of what has been accomplished. Will the accomplishment appear to have evaporated, in a slightly altered context? Has a new schema really been laid down, a new *analogon* stored for future trial, or will there be several rediscoveries later on before the logical pathway is really cleared? One investigation commits us to many more. Do we measure the swing of a pendulum in from the extremes? Again, we can. Of a heavy bob and a light bob, will the heavy one swing out *farther* on the other side? What is a pendulum doing when it is not swinging? (Under what conditions will the balance analogy, so inappropriate by gross visual analogies, be retrieved here?)

Of course, I do not wish to limit investigation to these kinds, where we are interested in the way humans construct taxonomies or road maps or networks (conceptual nets—it would beg many questions, at this stage, to call them "nomological"). But they are among the most important investigations, not only for education, but for epistemology in general. Significant concepts, concepts which reduce gross redundancy and bring order to our perception of the world, are not communicated, in the first instance, and thus cannot be 'taught.' This is the evidence of epistemology, from the time of Plato and Aristotle. A word can be taught, a name that will name a concept if it stands out for naming. But concepts can be *learned*, which means evolved in the economy of individual experience. Concepts of this order are not transmitted ready-made in the pulsed code of human communication, for they belong first to the apparatus which encodes and decodes those factual messages, not to the messages themselves. No one learns a first language by being 'told' it, he rather *abstracts* it from the rich parallel redundancy of two sorts of messages coming together: these from the natural, and those from the vocal, environment of his infancy. It is so likewise, I believe, with the later beginnings of scientific conceptualization: Such concepts as I speak of do not come first, and then serve to link and order the paths of experience; they grow, rather, as stopping places and intersections along paths of experience which, relative to them, are preconceptual. The process is as with the growth of cities; their highways create them.

The special importance of such investigations as I have been discussing—and epistemologically prejudging—is to describe, and fix vividly, the distinction between the evolution of conceptual expedients and the storage and recovery of single items of information in terms of already established conceptual habits. If we are going to talk about discovery in this conference, let us not forget that the word itself suffers from ambiguity of just the kind I have been discussing. This ambiguity is treated neatly by Stephen Toulmin (1953), who wrote a book on it. Most people, when they hear about a new scientific discovery, assume that what happened is like the discovery of a lost manuscript or a new continent or planet. But as Toulmin points out, many of the great discoveries, so called, are not like that at all. Einstein, for a famous example, did not find any new previously unknown entities or facts; what he found was a new way of classifying and relating known things, and this had the virtue of leading to predictions of *fact* which were new, discoveries in the second sense.

Toulmin illustrates what he means by the example of geometrical optics, which gives a uniform schematic representation of certain optical phenomena by finding an isomorphism between those phenomena and corresponding geometrical elements. The optical phenomena are not new; what is new is the ability to see them as elements in a geometrical pattern.

I am sure that Toulmin overdoes the contrast, or at least under-does the rich historical interconnections between new fact and new vision, each facilitating the other. But the contrast is still essential. In the elementary school context, we have seen Toulmin's particular example enacted more than once with the varied phenomena of light and shadow. It is not true that children first have all the facts straight, so to say, and then get the geometrical counterpart. And it is most emphatically not true that they can first get the geometry, and then anticipate the optics. A dominant group do not have the 'facts' straight at all, even up to gross errors in predicting where shadows will intersect things (surprisingly, this incompetence includes not a few adults). Their usual ability to summon forth the dubious statement, Light Travels in Straight Lines helps not at all. What one sees always is the intercommunication of fact and framework, of model and modeled.

In my discussion so far my main point has been the need to create, reproduce, and describe essentially complex and metastable states of momentary readiness for learning or evolving some rudimentary but powerful conceptual tools of science and thus the need of optimal teaching as a tool of investigation. It is my contention that the serious inquirer into learning at this level is almost committed, for the sake of knowledge, to become an educational reformer *malgré lui*.

Let me now come to the specific claims, hypotheses, or hunches suggested by the slogan, 'Discovery Method.' I shall be quick to say I react negatively to it, partly because I have already seen it used as a defense against a lack of subject content and as a way of minimizing the importance of preparation—of plowing, sowing, cultivating, irrigating—as against harvesting. Discovery Method suggests that teachers car harvest without the long preparation; and that notion can only, I think, take us back to the food-gathering stage, with thin crops indeed. If I were free to define from scratch, intending it to be a eulogistic term, I would say it was an attempt to teach with minimum self-deception about the powers of the spoken or printed word.

The crucial theoretical issue, as I see it, is an issue of cognitive psychology. It is an issue over the way we conceptualize what goes on in educationally significant learning. It is an issue, specifically, over the inherent simplicity or complexity of such learning, its inherent dependence on the cognitive history of the learner, and the kind and degree of autonomy exhibited by such a learner when he does learn or, to use an Aristotelian expression, the autotelic character of his operation.

This issue ought to be sharply distinguished from any overall debate about better and worse ways of teaching, although it has great relevance obviously. Arguments from theory to method are likely, at this stage, to be nonsequiturs. As said above, the best arguments seem likely, for some time, to run the other way. The notion that there is a single best way of teaching, across the universe of individual differences, of histories of preparation, of age, of teachers, is highly implausible. Still, there are directions indicated. One of them is typified by an old and well-known experiment of Edward Tolman, representing a type of study which psychologists have been too quick, I believe, to dismiss: latent learning experiments with rats. I bow for the moment to their authority concerning the rat, but not concerning the man. I have seen and heard reported too much of the same kind of human learning, sometimes, to minimize its importance, called play without directors and enticers. And that minimizing is what our schools have tended to do, almost to the vanishing point. But I should also make another claim, an a priori one in relation to the psychology of learning. This has to do with the inherent structural features of the adult world of science into which we propose to induct children. The order of this world is more complex than can be represented by the topology of linear orderings, or even of branching trees. It is inherently a network, a network of experimental paths intersecting at knots or nodes of significant conceptualization. We map this network, or try to, into linear orderings when we go marching through the curriculum, the 'little racecourse.'

We ourselves do not know the multiplicity of paths —which is one of the reasons why teaching cannot be separated from the arts and heuristics of discovery. What we do know, from the theory and history of knowledge, is that in exploring and mapping such a domain the fundamental metric is not feet or miles but an informational measure in psychological space, such that a well-trodden path is in principle a short one, and the path always long to what is new. The economy of slowing down, even wandering, lies in the creation of highways. When we say that a particular curricular involvement has, for certain children, a lot of mileage, we literally mean a large reduction of redundancy, and this could properly be called 'bittage" instead of 'mileage.' But variances of personal constitution and history will never allow a teacher to lead a child by his shortest paths unless the teacher directs himself toward a reinforcement of the child's autonomy, and thus in leading well is also led.

If there is any cogency in my argument, it suggests that the most promising scientific methodology in the study of learning and teaching is not that of the compact experiment, an image from the physical sciences. Nature simply doesn't scale that way. It seems to me entirely likely, indeed, that even the investigation of complex automata will soon reach beyond the paradigm of the neatly isolated system with its independent and dependent variables clearly labeled, with a few intervening ones grudgingly conceded; we won't design them for predictability but for evolution, ours as well as theirs. Yet, surely all such systems are gross and stilted when compared to the human child.

Chapter II

Variables in Discovery Learning

ROBERT GLASER

THE QUESTION ASSIGNED TO MY CONSIDERATION ASKS, IS LEARNING BY DIS-covery an important principle in curriculum development? I approach this task as someone concerned with the design of educational practice. I am interested in the requirements and specifications for the development of procedures and materials for discovery learning. As an educational designer, I work as a technologist, supplied with a presently meager, but apparently increasing, body of technological principles and practices. These are emerging from the interplay between practical attempts at education and relevant research and knowledge from the sciences which contribute to pedagogical methods.

My design orientation provides me with the following plan of operation: First, I must analyze the behavior with which I am concerned and specify some performance which will represent a standard of competence to be attained at the end of a sequence of educational experiences. This performance specification establishes a model or standard around which individual differences will be displayed. The selected performance must be specified in terms of its class properties because the stimulus, response, and structural characteristics of the subject-matter content and the behavioral repertoires involved will determine what I wish to teach and, correspondingly, how it is to be taught. I should not be too rigid, however, in sticking to an early specification of this performance because certainly the selection of my instructional goals will be influenced by my analysis of the behavior under consideration.

Second, I need to specify the characteristics of the students I am to teach. These characteristics need to be determined either prior to instruction or in the process of early learning. I shall need to know the extent to which the student has already acquired some of the things to be learned, the extent to which he has the prerequisites for learning the next instructional steps, the extent to which antecedent learning facilitates or interferes with new learning under the conditions I have in mind, and the extent to which an individual can make the necessary sensory discriminations and exhibit motor skills required for initial learning steps.

With information about both the target performance to be attained and the existing preinstructional behavior, I can proceed from one state to the other. This sets up my third task, which is to guide the student or allow him to go from one state of development to another, and I must construct the procedures and materials that I wish to employ in this educational process. As part of this process, I must make provisions for motivational effects, by which I mean providing conditions which will result in the maintenance and extension of the competence being taught.

Finally, I must make provision for assessing and evaluating the nature of the competence achieved by the learner in relation to the performance criteria that have been established.

If this description of the educational process sounds harshly technological, perhaps some elegance has been lost in analysis. But, presumably, once the basic techniques are designed, it is time for the practitioner to apply all the artistry and sensitivity he can muster.

In this paper I will consider only the *first step* of the *first task*, i.e., the general examination of the behavior under concern prior to an experimental analysis.

I cannot emphasize enough the importance of this first task—the analysis of behavior. I believe that it has been neglected in psychological research, and I also believe that it has been the most important element in recent improvements in instruction. In the design of educational programs, analyses of the terminal objectives to be achieved have been a more influential endeavor than manipulations in methods of teaching these objectives. This is probably so because it is the first step in the sequence of tasks in instructional design. (The fascination of Piaget and the Geneva School lies, to some extent, in their keen analyses of children's behavior; but they stop short of the succeeding steps in the operational plan for instruction.)

My analysis begins with an examination of the tasks that have been labeled discovery learning. I find here that I am confronted by a confusion between two different kinds of events. One has to do with learning *by* discovery, that is, teaching certain objectives by a discovery method; the other has to do with learning *to* discover, or teaching for a terminal objective which is manifested by the ability to make discoveries.

LEARNING BY DISCOVERY

The most prevalent case, learning by discovery is defined usually as teaching an association, a concept, or rule which involves 'discovery' of the association, concept, or rule. This is contrasted with a more direct instructional sequence in which a discovery method is not employed. And there are variations between these two. When one examines the task situations and instructional sequences that have been called discovery and those that have been contrasted with discovery, what are the outstanding features? Two differences are apparent: First, a learning-by-discovery sequence involves induction. This is the procedure of giving exemplars of a more general case which permits the student to induce the general proposition involved. Assessment of attainment is accomplished by testing whether the student has indeed induced the general proposition by getting him to verbalize it, getting him to apply it to certain exemplars in a way that indicates that he knows the general proposition, or by getting the student to generate additional exemplars. Finding the structure in a body of subject-matter instances is an example of induction, and the structure eventually discovered is a general proposition characterizing or summarizing the properties of these instances.

Second, in using the discovery method, the imposition of a structured instructional sequence is minimized in order to provide a relatively unguided sequence onto which the individual imposes his own structure. This kind of sequence, of necessity, allows the student to pursue blind alleys and find negative instances; and consequently, he makes some wrong moves or incorrect responses in the process of learning. Discovering implies a low probability of making a successful response. Such being the case, errors have a high probability of occurrence.

Discovery sequences can generally be characterized by these two properties: one, inductive sequences, and, two, trial and error or errorful learning in various degrees.

We should then examine these two processes: induction and errorful learning. Depending upon the behavioral objectives these processes are to teach, that is, whether they are to result in the establishment of associations, a concept, a rule, or generalization, these processes can be considered in different ways and can have different merits. However, before considering them with respect to particular terminal behaviors, it is of some use to discuss them generally.

Induction

I begin with the *contrast* to induction first. This is a teaching sequence in which a rule is presented before exemplars or instances of the rule. This is expository teaching, and in early work with programmed sequences, a rule–example–incomplete example sequence, appeared to be an excellent method for the efficient introduction of a new rule

(Evans, Homme, and Glaser, 1962). The rule–example–incomplete example presentation has the student working on the example of a new rule very early in his exposure to it. In this sort of sequence, the student is given an explicitly stated rule and one or more carefully chosen examples before being asked for a response to an incomplete example. An effective prompt is then set up which minimizes incorrect responses and which provides the student with the reinforcing activity of directly using the rule. Implied here is the rationale that rather than run the risk (at least in the fixed sequence of early program formats) of having the student induce an incorrect rule, it is preferable to state the rule for him explicitly. This philosophy leads to the rejection of inductive presentation. With a rule-example sequence, the student can recognize and apply a rule with proficiency, and often it seems hazardous and slow to approach a rule through induction or through incidental learning. With rule and then example, the student adopts the expert's carefully chosen statement of a rule rather than using his own more fallible induction-derived statement. The limited range of exemplars in most teaching and textbook situations may make it possible for the student to induce what is essentially an incorrect rule but one which happens to fit all the examples presented. This is another possible source of danger in the induction process.

The rule-example expository sequence just described is very frequently used in education. A teacher will typically enunciate a principle and follow this with a series of instances of the principle. This is a prevalent procedure because it leads to quick reinforcement for the teacher and the student. They both see close-to-critrion behavior occur rapidly. It is reinforcing, perhaps for the same reason that the use of punishment is reinforcing to the teacher—because it brings quick results. Other means of influencing behavior are more laborious and their results show up only in the long run.

Presenting rules first is also very effective because it is more useful to remember a general statement that mammals are warm-blooded animals and bear their young live than it is to remember that each specific species, such as monkeys, horses, cows, cats, dogs, etc. is a mammal (Mechner, 1961). Similarly, it is more useful to remember that the square of any number ending in 5 is equal to x times $(x + 1)$ followed by 25, than it is to remember the squares of specific numbers. In general, one is better off remembering information when it is stored in condensed abstract form rather than in many specific instances. The general statement is often the first one given in teaching because it is easiest to remember and because defining and presenting an adequate sample of instances is a difficult task. Sometimes examples of a general case have little dignity and statement of the rule is more profound. It is often easier, more dignified, and more productive of instant knowledge to state the rule before giving examples. While the words I use here suggest negative emotional loadings, nevertheless, for some purposes and for teaching certain kinds of tasks, rule-example is quite effective.

Consider now inductive teaching. Francis Mechner (1961) lucidly points out that great teachers and great writers know the principles of inductive teaching intuitively. Their writings provide us with demonstrations of the effectiveness of giving examples *before* rules. LaFontaine teaches a code of ethics through a series of allegorical fables. Shaw, in *Adventures of the Black Girl in Her Search for God*, makes a general point by providing a succession of specific instances which permit the reader to induce the general concept. Interestingly, Shaw's episodes describe noninstances of the concept being established: Moses, Freud, Pavlov, and others are instances of what God is not, and through these examples Shaw conveys his message.

Good writers ingeniously use a series of incidents to establish the concept of a character. It is hard work, at least for me, to read through the development of a Dostoevsky character so that the concept of this character emerges. C. P. Snow, with an inferior literary style, reinforces me more quickly because he tells me that Arthur Brown is this kind of a character—I get the rule first. Induction is also used by poets and composers when they develop general concepts by specific examples of images and themes.

In summary, it is a long-standing procedure, recognized in society for its excellence, that concepts and principles are learned by the presentation of specific instances which permit the learner or the recipient to generalize among specific instances of a class and to discriminate between instances and noninstances of a class. In these sequences of induction, the learner makes some false inductions, errors if you will, in the course of inducing the rule. Depending upon the subject matter, some rules can be pretty definitively learned, that is, subject to little further correction, such as inducing the concept of equality in mathematics. Other inductive sequences are subject to constant emendation or revision, such as the personality of a character in a story or such scientific concepts as force, energy, or the electron.

This inductive procedure is somewhat similar to the way we teach a concept according to the notions of Hull, Skinner, Keller and Schoenfeld, and, I suspect, Piaget. To teach a child the concept of redness, we first insure that the child has a relevant response available, in this case, that he can already say the word 'red.' However, he does not yet use it appropriately. (It is not under appropriate stimulus control.) The teaching sequence might point to a succession of pictures or objects asking each time, What color is this? Every time the child gives the right answer, he is provided with some event or context which provides confirmation or other reinforcement. The teacher or teaching sequence does not give the rule by pointing to objects and saying this is red, this is green, etc. The child is permitted to make responses by himself to the separate instances. The teaching sequence utilizes various kinds of red objects so that the student is provided with a succession of situations in which a correct response has a high probability of occurrence. Sequences of noninstances or negative instances are employed in which nonred (or possibly the color of the nonred object) is accepted as an appropriate response. The teaching procedure is careful to randomize the nonrelevant dimensions involved so that there are included large and small objects, distant and near objects, dark and light objects, and coarse and smooth objects. The child thus learns to generalize among objects in the class of redness. In the course of this process, the teaching sequence might introduce obviously different colors asking which one is blue and so on. Once the child says red only to red objects and not to nonred objects, and blue only to blue objects, he has acquired and perhaps discovered the concepts of redness and blueness.

In summary, then, the principle is that an abstraction or general case is learned by the establishment of generalizations among specific instances of a class and the discriminations between instances and noninstances of a class. In learning the concepts of triangle and quadrilateral, the student must generalize the reponse 'triangle' to any three-sided figure and the response 'quadrilateral' to any four-sided figure. He must also learn to discriminate between these two classes. In larger sequences of topics, a student learns what an operation is after he can add, subtract, multiply, etc. He learns what a proof is after he has seen a large number of different kinds of proofs. And he understands what homeostasis is after he learns about different kinds of physiological equilibria. General understanding is induced from a wealth of inexperience with specific cases (vide Mechner, 1961).

Errorful Learning

The second identifying characteristic of discovery learning is that in the course of discovering things for themselves, students will undoubtedly make mistakes as a result of exploring blind alleys and negative instances. Since it seems that the most intellectually satisfying discoveries are those which are not obvious from the data at the student's immediate disposal, there is the probability that such discoveries will not be made. To this extent, there may be a basic incompatibility between inducing discoveries and minimizing error.

To begin with a contrast again, the development of teaching machines has emphasized the minimization of errors. And while, so far as I know, completely errorless learning has not been demonstrated in a teaching machine program, it has been demonstrated in the ingenious work reported by Terrace (1963a; 1963b) in teaching pigeons a red-green discrimination, and also to discriminate between a horizontal and a vertical line. An error is defined in this work as a response to a stimulus correlated with nonreinforcement, a so-called S—. The results of these studies indicate that performance following discrimination learning without errors lacks three characteristics that were found following learning with errors. Only those birds that learned the discrimination with errors show (1) 'emotional' responses in the presence of S—, (2) occasional bursts of responses to the incorrect stimulus, and (3) less effective transfer to related discriminations. The technique Terrace used was to begin with two stimuli, widely separated on three stimulus dimensions, and then to progressively reduce the differences between two dimensions, maintaining only the difference in the third. This technique was recognized by William James in a discussion of discrimination in psychophysics in 1890.

Schlosberg and Solomon (1943) reported a study in which they trained rats on a Lashley jumping stand in a black-white discrimination. In order to equate for what they call the "negative factor" which prevents learning and increases response latency, they permitted no errors to occur which would be punished. In this way the value of the negative factor would be determined only by the distance to be jumped and hence equal for all stimulus presentations. They trained their animals very gradually in positive responses to a white stimulus so that an error was never made. As a result of this procedure, the experimenters say that "the gradient established by reward was uncomplicated by the effects of 'punishment'" (p. 26).

As Terrace points out, the demonstration of errorless learning suggests possible revision in currently accepted accounts of discrimination learning. These currently accepted accounts agree that the extinction of responding to S—, and hence the occurrence of errors, is a necessary condition for formation of a discrimination. As succinctly stated by Keller and Schoenfeld, "Extinction is the hallmark of discrimination" (1950). The accounts of Spence and Hull on discrimination

19

learning are similarly based upon learning that occurs in the presence of S+ and extinction in the presence of S−, respectively. Harlow (1959) expressly incorporates error in his error factor theory. In general, discrimination learning without errors is excluded fom these conditioning-extinction theories where excitatory and inhibitory gradients are postulated.

The general rationale for error minimization in instruction is the following: (1) When errors occur, there is lack of control over the learning process and opportunity is provided for the intermittent reinforcement of incorrect responses; this results in interference effects highly resistant to extinction. (2) Frustration and emotional effects, difficult to control, are associated with extinction and interference. And (3) richer learning, that is, richer in associations, takes place when the associative history of the learner is employed to extend his learning; this is accomplished by mediators or thematic promptings which make positive use of existing knowledge and serve to guide learning.

There is, perhaps, another reason behind the drive to minimize errors. This is the fact that the use of errors and the possible value of incorrect responses has not been investigated much in studies of learning related to the educational process. The contingencies generally studied have been those following correct responding—a reinforcing event, a punishing event, or withholding a reinforcing event. The contingencies following an incorrect response that have been studied are primarily punishment, withholding reinforcement, and to some extent, variations of corrective feedback information. This latter contingency has not, however, been as systematically investigated as the others. Recent experimental studies like those of Suppes and Ginsberg (1962) suggest that overt correction of errors in young children results in faster learning than does just knowledge about whether or not responses were correct. Although with adults, Suppes points out, studies like that of Burke, Estes, and Hellyer (1954) show that requiring the learner to make an overt correction response after informational feedback does not increase learning rate nor asymptotic performance. (Indeed, many learning studies assume, e.g., Bower (1962), that under certain conditions, correction following an incorrect response has reinforcing value equal to confirmation following a correct response.) In general, the 'guided' aspects of studies of guided discovery attempt to make use of error, but effective use requires development of theory and data about the function of error responses.

An exception to the lack of use of error responses in the course of instruction has been the work reported by Lewis and Pask on adaptive